TRAVEL

TRAVEL

Blythe Camenson

VGM Career Horizons
a division of NTC Publishing Group
Lincolnwood, Illinois USA

Photo Credits:
Pages 15 and 29: Photo Network, Tustin, CA; page 57: Baptist Mid-Missions.
All other photographs courtesy of the author.

Library of Congress Cataloging-in-Publication Data

Camenson, Blythe.
    Career Portraits, travel / Blythe Camenson.
       p.   cm. — (VGM's career portraits)
    Includes index.
    ISBN 0-8442-4365-5
    1. Tourist trade—Vocational guidance—Juvenile literature.
    [1. Tourist trade—Vocational guidance. 2. Vocational guidance.]
    I. VGM Career Horizons (Firm) II. Title. III. Series.
    G155.5.C36 1995   94-43362
    338.4'791023—dc20   CIP
                                                AC

Published by VGM Career Horizons, a division of NTC Publishing Group
4255 West Touhy Avenue
Lincolnwood (Chicago), Illinois 60646-1975, U.S.A.

5 6 7 8 9 QB 9 8 7 6 5 4 3 2 1

Contents

My heart is warm with the friends I make,
And better friends I'll not be knowing;
Yet there isn't a train I wouldn't take,
No matter where it's going!

Edna St. Vincent Millay
Travel

Introduction

Ever since the beginning of history, people have felt the urge to explore and travel. The early Greeks and Romans, the Vikings, Christopher Columbus, Marco Polo, Magellan, and many more curious and brave explorers ventured into unknown waters, learning about the world and carrying the information home with them. Early American settlers blazed trails across the United States, and modern-day astronauts rocket into space, studying the universe.

For many people today, the desire to travel is still as strong. Day-to-day life can become routine, but on a trip as far away as a foreign country, or as close to home as the next city or state, each experience is unique—visiting new places, trying new foods, and meeting new people.

Most people can travel only on their vacations, but some lucky individuals can travel more regularly as a part of their job.

On the following pages you will learn about many of the different careers that can take you on exciting adventures. So, buckle up your seat belts and enjoy the trip!

TRAVEL
WRITER

T ravel writers provide an important service. Just as the early explorers brought home information about the new lands they discovered, writers share what they see and experience with the rest of the world. They write magazine and newspaper articles, travel brochures, and travel guides. They help people make choices about where to take their vacations and also bring distant parts of the world to those unable to travel.

1

What it's like to be a travel writer

Travel writers know how to seek out interesting and unusual places and events, and they have the skill to capture what they see in print. A suitcase or briefcase functions as their office; portable typewriters, laptop computers, and tape recorders are their office equipment.

Some travel writers work as "freelancers," selling their stories to a variety of magazines or newspapers. Others work "on staff" and are employed permanently by a specific magazine, newspaper, or advertising or public relations agency.

Travel writers generally work and travel alone and have to be independent and self-sufficient. They are as familiar with the inside of an airport as they are with their computers or typewriters. And they must know how to handle any problems that could arise away from home.

What a travel writer does

There are several different kinds of travel articles. A service article might help readers choose the best luggage or give tips on how to travel with pets. A destination piece will take a general look at a city or country, giving information on how to get there and suggesting sights to see, restaurants and hotels. A third type of article zooms in on a specific angle, covering, for example, the architecture or history of a district, a famous person who might have lived there, or an unusual event that occurs there.

A travel writer uses every opportunity to find something of interest to document. Even an event or neighborhood close to home can provide material for an entertaining story.

The pleasures and pressures of the job

Freelance travel writers often have the freedom to pick their own destinations, and can choose when and how much they work. Being one's own boss has many advantages. The biggest disadvantage, however, is that paychecks don't come in on a regular basis and the amount earned can vary from story to story. Writers working on staff might not be able to choose where they travel, but they receive a regular salary.

Both freelancers and those employed permanently have to produce high-quality work. They have editors to report to and deadlines to meet. And sometimes things can go wrong. Planes are delayed, or the weather could refuse to cooperate.

Many writers love to see their "byline"—their name in print—giving them credit for the article. And to writers, nothing is more exciting than the finished product, getting to see their stories in print.

The rewards, the pay, and the perks

Salaries vary depending upon whether you're employed full-time or you're a freelancer selling one story at a time. Sometimes, the same article can be sold to more than one magazine or newspaper. These "resales" help to increase salaries. Also, you can be paid additional money if you provide your own photographs to illustrate your articles.

Getting started

In addition to a love of travel, travel writers must love the written word. They have to be skilled writers and understand what elements make a story special or interesting. Although attending college is not necessary, it's a good place to learn the basics of writing. Writers also improve their craft by attending seminars, lectures, and workshops and by reading what others writers write. Sometimes a travel writer also must know how to take his or her own photographs.

Freelance writers don't need a long, impressive resume to sell their first article. But to get a full-time, permanent position, or regular assignments from a publication, they must have a portfolio of "published clips" showcasing their best work.

Climbing the career ladder

Writers can progress from doing single articles to writing books. They can move up within a publication to become editors. Editors write articles and columns, but their main responsibility is to supervise the overall layout of the magazine or newspaper section.

Travel writers also can branch out and cover other specialties. A travel writer might write articles about history or careers, or switch to fiction and write mysteries and adventure stories.

Things you can do to get a head start

The easiest way to start is to explore your own hometown. Search out an activity about which you think readers in another part of the country would like to learn. Does your town have a special country fair or an unusual art exhibit? How about early settlers or famous literary figures? Are any of their houses still standing, perhaps as a museum open to the public?

And be sure to read what other writers are doing. You can examine travel magazines and newspaper travel sections at your library. The library is a good place to find history and background information and stimulate story ideas.

Let's Meet...

Valerie Vaz
Travel Writer/Editor

Valerie Vaz is Senior Associate Editor of Contemporary Living at *Essence* magazine, which reaches more than 5 million African-American women readers.

How did you get started in journalism?

I started at the copy desk at *Time* magazine, and then I moved into an internship there in economy and business. I thought it was going to be boring at first, but it was during the market crash of 1986 and it turned out to be very exciting. Later I worked at *Money* magazine and then I came to *Essence* in 1989. It was a chance to have more responsibility and independence, to handle a story from the idea to the finish. When I started out there were certain things I wanted to do. I was interested in travel and travel writing, and entertainment reporting about the film industry, and news. I've always had an interest in what's going on in the world.

What are your duties at *Essence* magazine?

I'm in charge of the Contemporary Living section. In addition to travel writing and travel editing, I'm responsible for editing the

parenting section. I also work with the food editor on stories and recipes. I love to cook.

As the travel editor I assign stories to staff or freelance writers. I also travel and write stories myself. I've been to a variety of places on assignment–Zimbabwe, Ghana, Canada, Jamaica, Hawaii, St. Lucia, and Barbados.

What advice would you give to someone considering travel writing as a career?

When you go someplace, whether to camp or on a vacation with your parents, I think it's a good idea to keep a journal. Take notes. Talk to people and find out what they think is interesting about where they live. Find out what they like to do. And observe and feel everything around you and then put that into words.

What do you like most/least about your job?

What I like most is getting to be in new places, meeting new people, revisiting places that I love, learning new things, and expanding my horizons. I enjoy working with writers, discussing ideas and how to approach a story, as well as helping them shape and polish their pieces. The downside is that I don't get to stay as long as I would like in a place. The time is limited and you can end up feeling rushed. And on a trip I end up spending too much time handling administrative things— arranging interviews, coordinating with photographers. Another difficult aspect of my job is having to turn down writers who want to submit stories to the magazine. We just don't have enough space to run everything.

Valerie on Assignment

While on assignment in Zimbabwe, Valerie Vaz wrote a letter home about her impressions.

October

Dear Mom,
  Here I am in Zimbabwe, working on the article, "Ten Proud Years of Freedom." I've been running around interviewing people for the story. I've talked to artists, singers, and writers. I even met President and First Lady Mugabe.
  I've also had time to catch glimpses of some of the most beautiful places on earth—a game park with all sorts of wild animals and Victoria Falls, which is an amazing sight.
  I even got a chance to have a traditional home-cooked meal. I copied down the recipes for the magazine's Food Section.
  And I didn't forget you, Mom. I picked up a little native sculpture for you. See you soon.
  Love,
      Valerie

Let's Meet...

Thomas Swick
Travel Writer/Editor

Thomas Swick started in journalism in 1977 and has been a travel editor for a major newspaper since 1989. He is the author of the book *Unquiet Days: At Home in Poland*.

Tell us how you got started.

I was always interested in travel, and in high school I got interested in writing, so it was just a natural combination of the two things I felt most passionate about. I spent my last summer of college working in London. I studied in France for a year and then lived abroad for a few years, particularly in Poland, and I wrote about those experiences.

What schooling or training would someone need to get into the profession?

I don't think you need to necessarily study journalism. I majored in literature in college and I read a lot of travel books and I traveled. Journalism you can learn by doing; but history, or any of the arts, is a good background to have.

How competitive is it to get a job on a newspaper, and then work your way up to travel editor?

It is competitive. First of all, it's difficult getting jobs in newspapers these days because there are fewer newspapers. With travel jobs it varies. At some papers, the travel editor position is still the job they give the old-timer before he retires, as a plum reward for all those years of service. And with other papers, there's a lot of competition because it's such an enjoyable job and everyone wants it.

Why is the job so enjoyable? What do you like best?

I like the variety. The three main things I do are travel, write, and edit freelance stories that writers send in to the paper. I like planning the section and being able to reflect my personality in it. I like being able to educate and entertain people, which is what I try to do in my articles.

What do you like the least?

Probably the time constraints, having to put a section out every week. It's a lot of work and you can never relax. There can be a lot of pressure. If I'm away on vacation or on assignment, I have to write the articles and plan the section in advance before I go, so it's double or triple the work. The bigger papers usually have a couple of people in the department, but in my situation, there's no one else there, no assistant editor.

Also, I think that travel sections need to inform people about bargains and trips and tours and things like that—but I don't like it when public relations people are pushy and insist that I run something about their hotel, their resort, or their package tour.

A Day in the Life of a Travel Editor

Many people think that life as a travel editor is nothing but glamour; Tom Swick wrote this tongue-in-cheek column to set them straight.

8:30   Five-minute drive to work. Think of future column topics. One possibility: driving to work.

8:38   First person I pass in hallway says, "What are you doing here so early?"

8:45   Log onto computer and check wire service to scan stories on Fiji, Edinburgh, and traveling with kids. Spend next 10 minutes typing the number 1 in front of all the area codes.

9:33   Food editor asks to borrow atlas.

9:35   Reader calls. Says we ran something, sometime within the past five years (I've been here three) on either a hotel or a bed and breakfast, in either the southeast or the northwest, that welcomes pets. Do I remember the name? Thinks it begins with a "B."

10:00 Editorial assistant flings freelance piece on Italy at me. Begin editing it.

10:50 Retrieve mail. Most addressed to someone else, or to Mr. Switch, Mr. Swift, or Mr. Sick. Freelance submissions include one story titled: "Canada is Many Things." (Still not as good as the ex-food editor's favorite: "Pity the Poor Pickle.")

11:30 Feature writer asks to borrow atlas.

12:00 Pizza at Sal's. I try to live up to my title by always going out to lunch.

1:15   Call travel agent about tickets to Des Moines.

1:40   Medical writer asks to borrow atlas.

2:00   Finish editing Italian story. Harried reporter passes, says, "Where you off to now? Oh, Italy. Must be nice."

2:15   Finally start writing column!

Success Stories

Paul Theroux

Paul Theroux, a prolific writer, began seeing his novels in print in 1966. Sales were slim, though, until 1975 when his travel book, *The Great Railway Bazaar: By Train Through Asia,* was released. It has the distinction of being one of the few travel books to ever become a bestseller in this country. Many more followed as Theroux continued exploring the world by train. Some of his successes include *The Mosquito Coast, Riding the Iron Rooster by Train through China, Sailing through China,* and *Kingdom by the Sea: a Journey around Great Britain.*

Theroux was born in Massachusetts and studied at the Universities of Massachusetts and Maine. He has traveled extensively, to almost every continent on the globe, both as a writer and as an English teacher. He has homes in England and Cape Cod.

Caribbean Travel and Life

Caribbean Travel and Life was established in 1985 and is a bimonthly magazine covering travel to the Caribbean, Bahamas, and Bermuda. Although its editors prefer to work with established writers, it would not be impossible for a newcomer to break in. The magazine buys about 30 manuscripts a year from freelancers as well as photos to illustrate the articles.

Find Out More

The ten sins of travel writing

Travel editor Thomas Swick has provided a checklist of what to avoid in a travel article. With these in mind, do you think you could be a good travel writer?

1. __All travel stories sound the same. Try to find something new to say about a place. What amused you, depressed you, or intrigued you?

2. __They are filled with cliches. Avoid the "Mexico: Land of Contrasts!" school of writing. Find a more creative way to say things.

3. __They tell instead of show. Don't *tell* readers that people are friendly or that a city is beautiful. *Show* them through an anecdote or well-observed details.

4. __They try to cover too much. Choose a narrow focus for your story.

5. __They gush. Notice the unexpected things and present them calmly, without fuss.

6. __They ignore the people. How can you understand a place without understanding the people who live there? Include some dialogue in your story.

7. __They are superficial. Most travel stories just scratch the surface. Dig deeper.

8. __They are humorless. Travel is rich in comedy. Make your readers laugh.

9. __They lack continuity. A good travel story should not be a series of random impressions. It should have a theme.

10. __They fail to enchant. Remember to convey the wonder of a place.

Find out more about travel writing

Society of American Travel Writers
1155 Connecticut Avenue
Suite 500
Washington, D.C. 20006

American Society of Journalists and Authors
1501 Broadway
New York, NY 10036

Market Guide for Young Writers.
Writer's Digest Books,
Lots of good advice for young writers from ages eight through eighteen, including tips on getting started, listings of buyers, how to submit material, payments, writing contests, and prizes.

TRAVEL
PHOTOGRAPHER

T he life of travel photographers is similar to that of travel writers. They travel extensively on assignment, capturing the special features of a place or event on film. A camera bag is their office; cameras, lenses, tripods, filters, and light meters are their office equipment.

Some travel photographers work as "freelancers," selling their photographs to a range of magazines, newspapers, or ad agencies. Others work "on staff" for one particular publication or agency.

15

What a travel photographer does

Photographers on assignment must meet the needs of the publication or agency for whom they are working. They search out scenic locales and plan in advance what they'll need to get that perfect picture. They might have to hire models or rent props, and in certain locations they might have to get permission from the appropriate authorities.

Photographers who are working with writers, or are writers themselves, often must tailor their pictures to the text of a specific article they will illustrate.

Many photographers also operate their own "stock" libraries. In the course of their travels, they collect a large number of photographs that they don't have immediate use for. These are available for rent to others who might be looking for a particular shot or subject. They might focus on standard landmarks such as San Francisco cable cars or the Tower of London, or they might photograph landscapes or people in their national dress.

The pleasures and pressures

Travel photographers not only get to see the world, they're able to document it. They go on safari in Africa, watch the dismantling of the Berlin Wall, trace the Silk Route through China, or follow the Tall Ships on their voyages. And though places might change over time, their photographs allow future generations to see the way things once were.

But it can be a tough job. There's a lot of heavy and expensive equipment to carry, film or cameras can get damaged, the weather can be bad, and it can be dangerous. During periods of political upheaval, some locations might not always be friendly toward visitors. But most photographers love their work and agree the advantages far outweigh any disadvantages.

The training you'll need

Some photographers are self-taught, while others attend college or art school. Still others find a photographer for whom they can apprentice.

You should become familiar with all the technical as well as artistic aspects of photography and study what other photographers produce. Also, it is helpful for photographers to know how to write. This will enable them to write their own articles to go with their pictures.

Branching out

Travel photographers can do commercial work—studio portrait work, fashion, or advertising photography. They can create travel posters, postcards, and calendars, or compile collections of photographs for coffee-table books.

Travel photographers also can teach their various skills to interested beginners. They instruct in evening school classes or speak at seminars and workshops.

The rewards, the pay, the perks

Payment varies from assignment to assignment and from publication to publication. Sometimes a photographer will be paid a set amount for each photograph that eventually sees print. That amount will vary depending on the size of the photograph; whether it, for example, fills a quarter, half, or full page. Photographs that make the cover of a magazine earn more.

Sometimes a photographer will work on an hourly or day rate. An editor might agree to pay for two full days of work at a set fee. If the assignment takes longer, the photographer will not earn any more money for that particular job. At the same time, if he spends less time than he planned, he is not expected to refund any of the fee.

In addition to their fee, photographers usually are paid for any additional expenses such as hiring models or renting extra equipment or props. And on assignment, travel expenses usually are covered as well.

Freelancers working "on spec" might have to pay their own travel expenses, air fare, hotel, meals, etc., then hope to sell enough photographs to be compensated adequately.

Getting started

A budding photographer needs only a simple camera and a keen eye. Study pictures published in magazines and books and look at the lighting and composition. Visit your library and browse through the magazines. Your library also can help you with "how-to" books to give you the basics.

Then go out and start shooting. Study your results and compare them to professional shots. Find a working photographer in your neighborhood and volunteer some time to assist him or her.

Let's Meet...

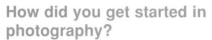

Bill Bachmann
Travel Photographer

Bill Bachmann has been a freelance travel photographer since 1977. His photographs have appeared in *Cosmopolitan, Vogue, Time, People, Travel & Leisure,* and many others.

How did you get started in photography?

It began as a hobby. Even though I minored in photography in college, I never really thought it would be a career. But I was studying in London for awhile and I was given an assignment to travel to Russia. It snowballed from there.

What schooling or training did you need to become a photographer?

Even though I went to college, you don't need formal training for this work. You learn on your feet, you learn by doing. And you need a good eye, an ability to really *see* and a good portfolio. No one asks you where you went to college.

If you were to start all over again, would you do anything differently?

I would still be a photographer, but instead of starting out on my own, I would find someone good to assist. That's the best way to learn, from someone already established.

Do you work alone or as part of a team?

It's always different. Sometimes I take models with me and big crews, assistants and makeup artists, and sometimes I'm by myself. It depends on the assignment.

What's the best part about your work?

I like not having any idea what's going to happen next. That excites me more than anything else. And that's why I prefer travel photography to studio work. Studio work can be too predictable.

What is the most difficult part of your job?

You can't plan your life too far ahead. If there's a concert I want to see, for example, I never know if I'll be in town or not. Also, there are hassles involved with travel. Customs officials, carrying the equipment, getting permissions, and dealing with all the different regulations in the various countries.

What assignment are you working on now?

I've been doing an extensive World Monument Tour for Kodak and Hilton Hotels, documenting the new Russia, China and Eastern Europe, in addition to much of the Middle East and Asia. It's a 170-day assignment, shooting all the major monuments including the Great Wall of China, the Great Buddha in Japan, the Great Pagoda in Thailand, and the pyramids of Egypt.

Some Memorable Moments for Bill Bachmann

When Bill was in East Berlin in the 70s, before the wall came down, photographing some of the ruins from World War II, all of a sudden he was being shot at–and not with cameras. Two men dressed in black started running after him, shooting their guns. They chased him for quite a distance. Bill dashed into a youth hostel and hid inside for twenty minutes or so, waiting for them to leave. Later, he developed his film hoping it would give him a clue as to what had caused this, but there was nothing. He could only assume he had been near some kind of secret operation and they thought he was a spy.

Another time, Bill was just finishing some work in Singapore, getting ready to leave to go to Japan. He started feeling ill and went to the hospital. It turned out his appendix had ruptured and instead of a 4-day stay, he ended up there for 18 days. He was all alone, no one from home knew where he was and no one spoke English, even the doctor. It was one of the worst experiences on location he's ever had.

But another experience made up for it. Bill was in Egypt just after the earthquakes in 1992 photographing the pyramids and mingling with the people. He had a military guard with him because at that time tourists were targets for terrorists, but still, he felt it was so wonderful experiencing that country, the camels, and the markets. And the people were incredible, too. They were living in little huts right next to the rubble, but you would never know they'd just been through a disaster. Their resiliency and ability to overcome the hardship was wonderful for Bill to watch. It was one of those times he felt overpoweringly happy with what he was doing.

Let's Meet...

Rita Ariyoshi
Travel Photographer

Rita Ariyoshi has been a travel photographer for more than twenty years. Her photos have appeared in the *New York Times*, *The Los Angeles Times*, and *Travel and Leisure*, among others.

What drew you to travel photography?

I started out as a travel writer. I would call my photographer friends to illustrate my stories for me, but they would end up making more money than I did. So I thought "I'm going to try this." My mother was an artist and I always painted with her so, just by osmosis, I had a fairly good grasp of composition.

Did you have any formal training?

For my first attempt at photography, I went with a press group that was invited to India. I asked a photographer friend what cameras and lenses I should have and off I went. The whole time I just acted like a dummy and kept asking these photographers, "What are you doing? Why are you doing that?" and it was like a month-long seminar to be with these people. I came back with saleable images.

Then I signed up for courses at a local college with a good darkroom and I also took Nikon's intensive weekend workshop. That's the basic training I had. Also, in my earlier position as a writer and editor (of *Aloha Magazine*) I had been buying photography, so I had a good idea of what worked and what didn't.

After learning the craft, what should a beginning photographer do to sell his or her work?

I already had a foot in the door because I had worked with the various magazine editors when I was writing articles. Concentrating on writing first is an excellent way to get started. Pairing writing and photography is one of the most successful things someone can do.

If you're not a writer you could start by building a stock base. That means going out to areas that have travel icons. For instance, Diamond Head, the Eiffel Tower, things like that. Get enough good pictures and then you can start to promote yourself. Buy a copy of the *Photographer's Market,* which lists publications and businesses that buy photos, and send your work out. Even though you might be using slide film, which is what you need to do in order to sell, when you send photos in on spec (speculation) you should pay the extra money to have 8 × 10 prints made. Editors might not take the time to examine slides carefully, but a couple of dramatic prints will capture their attention. Then let them know you have the slides to go with the prints. And always remember to enclose a SASE (stamped, self-addressed envelope) so you can get your work returned to you.

The Anatomy of an Assignment

Using a recent job for the *New York Times* as an example, Rita walks us through the steps of getting and executing a travel photography assignment.

1. The *New York Times* travel editor needed a shot of people bicycling around Oahu Bay.

2. She called me and we agreed upon a fee for my time, to pay for models, and to cover expenses. She also gave me a two-week deadline.

3. Knowing the area, I mentally pictured a few good, scenic places where I could position people on bicycles.

4. I enlisted the help of my son and his girlfriend, a young, attractive couple, to be my models.

5. I had only one bicycle, so I had to rent another one.

6. I loaded up the station wagon with all my equipment—the bicycles, my camera, an 80mm to 200mm telephoto lens, a 28mm wide-angle lens, a 35mm to 70mm wide-angle zoom, a tripod, and a ladder. The ladder served an important function. When you want to do something scenic, but you have two people on bicycles, they can block the scenery. By climbing a ladder and getting above the bicycles, I can have my models in the foreground and have all the scenery spread out behind them.

7. I decided to shoot in full sunlight because I didn't want a lot of shadows. We headed out around nine o'clock in the morning.

8. I drove to two different locations to give the editor a choice: a wild and wonderful stretch of coastline, and a funky little town on the north shore that's a surfing mecca.

9. On the beach I posed my models as if they had just pulled in and stopped, and in town I had them moving. For the action shot, I used a fast shutter speed of 500. My camera has a continuous focus so, as they moved across my line of vision, the camera kept the shots from blurring automatically.

10. I worked until about three o'clock, then sent the film to a professional lab to be developed.

11. My check arrived after I delivered the photos.

12. After another two weeks my photos appeared in print and the editor sent me a copy. She had chosen the exact two shots I thought she would and I was pleased with how they looked.

13. Even though I knew the *Times* would be converting the shots into black and white, I used color slide film so I could include the pictures in my stock library. I have sold those same shots more than a dozen times to other publications.

Success Stories

National *Geographic* *Magazine*

National Geographic Magazine is an illustrated monthly publication that was founded in 1888. It is well known for its beautiful photographs. A photographer who is able to land an assignment or sell a photo to *National Geographic* is considered both talented and lucky. Also, he or she will be well compensated.

The magazine covers travel, geography, science, exploration, and social problems, but unlike other large-circulation magazines, *National Geographic* is not found on newsstands. It can boast, however, of one of the largest annual circulations in the world with more than 11 million subscribers. A collector's item since its early days, subscribers save back issues for the maps and photographs. *National Geographic* was edited by Gilbert Hovey Grosvenor for more than fifty years and is published by the National Geographic Society.

Endless *Vacation*

Endless Vacation was established in 1974 and is read by more than 800,000 subscribers. Although it is a difficult magazine for a beginner to sell to, its editors do buy photographs and articles from freelancers. The magazine focuses on vacation health-related topics, weekend travel spots, travel trends, resorts, and upscale destinations. Articles must include up-to-date pertinent information with accurate costs, dates of events, names, addresses, and phone numbers.

The editors suggest writers and photographers study the magazine, then write to them to request their guidelines.

Find Out More

Find out more about travel photography

American Society of Media
    Photographers
14 Washington Road
Suite 502
Princeton Junction, NJ 08550

Photographer's Market.
Writer's Digest Books

A comprehensive listing of more than 2,500 U.S. and international buyers of freelance photographs. Each listing gives the name and address of the buyer, how to submit your photos, what kind of photos they buy, pay rates, and tips on how to break in.

*A Guide to Travel Writing &
    Photography.*
Writer's Digest Books

Introduces writers and photographers to the field of travel writing. Shows how to explore your interest in travel and earn money from it. With color photographs.

TRAVEL
AGENT

O ut of all the industries worldwide, travel and tourism continue to grow at an astounding rate. Nearly everyone tries to take at least one vacation every year and many people travel on business frequently. Some travel for education or for that special honeymoon or anniversary trip.

At one time or another, most travelers seek out the services of a travel agent to help with all the details of a trip. This means that jobs for travel agents will continue to grow. Travel agents learn about all the different destinations, modes of transportation, hotels, resorts and cruises, then work to match their customers' needs with the services travel providers offer.

What it's like to be a travel agent

Travel agents work in an office and deal with customers in person or over the phone. They plot itineraries, make airline and hotel reservations, book passage on cruise ships, or arrange for car rentals. They listen to the needs of their customers, then try to develop the best package for each person. They work with affluent, sophisticated travelers, or first-timers (such as students trying to save money and travel on a budget). Travel agents could book a simple, round-trip air ticket for a person traveling alone, or handle arrangements for hundreds of people traveling to attend a convention or conference.

Some travel agents are generalists; they handle any or all situations. Others specialize in a particular area, such as cruise ships or corporate travel.

How a travel agent gets the job done

Travel agents gather information from different sources. They use computer databases, attend trade shows, and read trade magazines. They also visit resorts or locations to get firsthand knowledge about a destination.

They have to keep up with rapidly changing fares and rates, and they have to know who offers the best packages and service. Their most important concern is the satisfaction of their customer.

Happy customers come back again and refer friends and family.

The pleasures and pressures of the job

Most travel agents are offered "fam" trips to help familiarize them with a particular cruise line, safari adventure, exclusive resort, or ecological tour. These trips are offered free to the travel agent so they can "test-drive" a destination before suggesting it to their customers. Travel providers understand that a travel agent is more likely to sell what he or she knows and has enjoyed. Travel agents also receive discounted travel on other business trips, as well as on their own vacations.

The downside, however, is that they seldom have enough free time to do all the traveling they would like. They often are tied to their desks, especially during peak travel periods such as the summer or important busy holidays. And the work can be frustrating at times. Customers might not always know what they want, or their plans can change, and as a result, the travel agent might have to cancel or reroute destinations that had been set already.

The rewards, the pay, the perks

Salary varies according to the region in which you work and your experience. Depending on the agency, you could start out on an hourly wage or a yearly salary. Some travel agents prefer to work on a commission basis. That way, the more trips they sell, the more money they earn. A salary plus commission is the best combination to work toward.

Travel agents who are good salespeople also can earn bonuses or more free or discounted trips. If your pay is initially low, it can be offset by this added benefit.

Getting started

A four-year college degree is not necessary to become a travel agent. It can be helpful, however, and shows commitment and discipline. Most travel agents study for at least two years and earn an associate's degree. Many community colleges, trade and vocational schools offer good programs in travel and tourism or hospitality management. Some travel agencies are willing to hire inexperienced applicants and provide them with their own training.

For a list of schools offering certified programs, you can write to the American Society of Travel Agents or the Institute of Certified Travel Agents. (Their addresses are listed at the end of this chapter.)

Things you can do to get a head start

In junior high and high school you need to stay awake during geography, history, and social studies classes, and to keep a good eye on the newspaper and the nightly news. It's important to have an understanding of what's happening in the world around you. This will not only help you learn how to sell a vacation, but it will help you to sell the right vacation. Informed travel agents make sure they don't send vacationers to an area of the world where there's a conflict going on.

Through public-speaking classes in school, you can gain self-confidence and become comfortable working with other people. It's also a good idea to get some retail sales experience. You could get a part-time job at the mall or do some telephone or customer relations work.

Travel agents are required to learn a computerized reservation system. You can start by becoming familiar with computers and data bases. Most important, you can start sharpening your listening skills.

Let's Meet...

Vivian Portela Buscher
Travel Agent

Vivian Portela Buscher started out as a ticket agent and in passenger services for the airlines, then moved to a well-known cruise line as a booking agent. She is now a travel agent specializing in cruise travel.

What made you decide to enter the travel industry?

That's an easy question. I like to travel. I enjoy being involved with jobs related to travel. It's easy for me to advise other people about travel because it's something I like to do.

I chose to be a travel agent because working with the airlines had been becoming more and more difficult. You had to wait a long time to gain seniority and to have a comfortable work schedule with Saturdays and Sundays off. Plus, with so many airlines going out of business, there are a lot of unemployed people in the industry. The airline I worked for folded ten years ago and I was happy to switch to the cruise business. I was looking for a job that would still be in the travel industry but that would be more secure and with normal hours.

What hours do you work?

I work Monday through Friday, and since our agency is open from

9:00 A.M. to 9:00 P.M., I get to choose my hours during the day. Most people prefer to work earlier hours, but I don't. Basically, I work from 10:30 A.M. to 7:00 P.M.

What special training did you need to be a travel agent?

When I went to college I studied air carrier management and received a bachelor's degree in transportation management. My experience with the airlines and then with the cruise line also was important in preparing me. The rest I picked up through on-the-job training.

How would you describe your job?

People call me who have an interest in taking a cruise vacation and I find them the right cruise, at the right price. I think of it more as a matching game rather than a selling situation. My office doesn't call anyone asking them to buy a cruise; every-one calls us.

What do you like most about your job?

I enjoy travel a lot and it's nice to be able to talk about it all day long and to help people find the right travel experience. There's a lot of satisfaction when someone calls me back and tells me that the cruise was exactly as I had described it, and that it was the best vacation of his or her life.

Getting the Job,
Starting the Job

Here is a description of how Vivian Portela Buscher landed her job and what the first day was like.

A friend of hers was offered the job first, but it wasn't the right location for her. She knew Vivian had the same background and experience, so she referred her to the agency. The operations manager interviewed Vivian over the telephone. He asked her about her background, and then told her he was very interested and asked if she could start right away.

An in-person interview was set for the next day, but because he already knew about her experience, he told her about the agency and what her duties and salary would be. Vivian began work one week later.

Her first day was hectic. The company has grown tremendously since she's been there, but at the time they were understaffed and the phones were ringing and they were just in the process of reorganizing the office. She walked in cold and they told her to start answering the phones. Vivian had no idea what she was supposed to say. At first she took the calls and passed messages on to the other agents. Then she started taking down more information, asking the customers what they needed, and started getting that information for them.

There was a lot of new information Vivian had to learn, and intensive studying she had to do to acquire all the product knowledge about all the different cruise lines and packages. It was busy for her, but exciting.

Let's Meet...

Mary Fallon Miller
Travel Agent

Mary Fallon Miller started her career as a travel agent in 1986 when she opened her own agency. She specializes in cruise travel.

How did you become interested in a career as a travel agent?

At the age of seven I sailed across the Atlantic on the S.S. *France,* and later, as a young woman, I accompanied my mother throughout Europe and South America. I fell in love with the glamour and excitement of travel. It gets in your blood; I have a real fascination for other cultures and languages. I realized that a career as a travel agent would allow me to pursue my dream to see more of the world.

Has it worked out that way? Have you had the time to travel?

When you're just starting out, you're tied to the office and the computer, but a newcomer would get to take at least one week a year. The owners of a travel agency get to go on more "fam" trips, but if someone just starting out is seen as a productive member of the business, helping to build it, he or she would get more opportunities.

What do you like most about being a travel agent?

Having a passenger or a guest that's happy. Having a family reunion done successfully, having a group of people come back over and over and recommend you to their friends. What could be more flattering?

What's the most difficult part of your job?

Keeping all the details accurate and being able to deal with what we call "grumps and whiners." There are people who get very nervous about their travel arrangements and they can complain and make your life miserable. But you have to be able to be compassionate–find out *why* they're so concerned. Maybe they had a bad experience in the past. You have to try to know as much about your client as possible.

And there are times when things go wrong. There could be a snow-in at an airport and people miss their connections or someone in the family dies and they have to cancel their whole cruise reservation at the last minute. You have to be professional, flexible, and on the ball all the time.

It's a demanding job, but it's satisfying. People come back and say, "I can't believe you knew exactly what I wanted. That's the best vacation I've ever had. And I'm telling all my friends." You start getting more and more customers coming in and they ask for you by name. That feels really good. You're making a dream come true, and in a way, that's what you're doing–selling dreams.

A Typical Day for Mary Fallon Miller

9:00   I return a phone call to Mr. and Mrs. Jones to tell them I was able to get them a great cabin. We discuss which seating time for dinner they prefer and I ask them if they're celebrating any birthdays. (If they are, the cruise staff will provide a birthday cake.) I let them know when they'll get their tickets and on what date their deposit is due.

9:30   A call comes in from a John and Sue who are getting married. They want to know about a hotel that provides a reception hall, and then they want me to book their flight to Aruba for their honeymoon.

10:00 I make a few phone calls to different hotels and the airlines, and then I call the couple back with confirmations.

11:00 Another couple telephones to ask if I can find them a resort that caters to young people. They want to go to the Virgin Islands and ask about passport requirements, and if they need any inoculations.

12:00 I make a few phone calls on their behalf to see what's available.

1:30   After lunch I do some research at my desk reading brochures, and trade magazines such as *Travel Weekly* and *Travel Agent*.

2:30   I confirm a few details on a cruise I booked the day before, then I begin work developing a roster list. One hundred people are traveling by bus to Miami, and then they'll hook up with their cruise. I have to make sure all their names are correct and that their hotel rooms are all booked.

4:00   IBM called to book a hotel for a convention. I have to take down all the details, how many rooms they'll need and for how many nights. We also discuss their budget and what we expect the cost to run. I spend the rest of the day contacting various hotels. I'll call IBM back in the morning to give them a few choices.

Success Stories

International Youth Hostel Federation

Travelers who join the International Youth Hostel Federation are able to stay at inexpensive dormitory-style youth hostels located in more than 50 countries around the world. The Federation has designed the hostels particularly for young people and students on hiking or biking tours. The hostels usually are located about 15 to 30 miles from each other and allow a stay of up to three nights. To obtain membership information and a handbook listing the locations of more than 4,500 hostels throughout the world contact: American Youth Hostels, Inc., 733 15th Street, N.W., Washington, D.C. 20036.

Henry Ford

Henry Ford popularized the automobile as a means of travel for the average American and created a major company that is still thriving today. Ford, as a young man, was fascinated by the promise of the internal combustion engine and the first car he designed and built in 1896 was a light carriage with a 2-cylinder engine. In 1908 he developed the Model T, which was priced at $850. Ten thousand were sold the first year; 15 million were sold by 1927 when production of the Model T ended.

Find Out More

You and a career as a travel agent

Below is a list of the qualities a good travel agent should possess. Check off all that apply to you.

__ Communication skills. You have to be able to listen well and understand the concerns and special needs of your customers.

__ An understanding of finances. You'll need to work on your math skills to handle billing and collecting funds for the various fares and reservations.

__ A people-person. The customer comes first. You need to be someone who is friendly and enjoys working with all types of people.

__ A problem solver. Arranging vacations and business trips can be like solving a big jigsaw puzzle. You have to be good at fitting all the pieces together.

__ Detail-oriented. There's a lot of detail work in the travel business. You have to be conscientious and remember to dot all your "i's" and cross your "t's."

__ Well-organized. You have to be able to recognize priorities and manage your time well.

__ A good researcher and studier. You have to read a lot and study the industry so you can match the client's desires with the best deals being offered.

__ Patience. No matter how good your intentions, things don't always run as smoothly as you would like. It's important not to get rattled easily.

Find out more about becoming a travel agent

American Society of Travel Agents
1101 King Street
Alexandria, VA 22314

Association of Retail Travel
  Agents
1745 Jefferson Davis Highway
Suite 300
Arlington, VA 22202

Institute of Certified Travel
  Agents
148 Linden Street
P.O. Box 56
Wellesley, MA 02181

CRUISE
STAFF

P robably everyone, at one time or another, has seen
reruns of "The Love Boat" on television and
watched Julie, Doc, Issac, Gopher, and Captain
Steubing go about their daily activities, interacting with
passengers while ensuring that they have the best vacations of their lives.

Although the reality might not exactly mirror life on
the popular series, being part of a cruise ship staff can be
fun and exciting. You will have the opportunity to travel

to exotic ports, meet all different kinds of people, make new friends, and lead a carefree lifestyle.

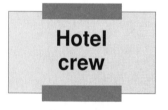

The different jobs aboard ship

Cruise lines employ all sorts of personnel to handle the many tasks involved with running a ship. A smaller ship with 850 passengers might have over 400 crew members; the larger ships that carry 2,500 or so passengers employ up to 1,000 crew members.

The "marine crew"–the captain, seamen, deck officers, oilers, engineering officers—generally come from the ship's point of origin, Greece, Norway, or Italy, for example, so most of the jobs open to Americans are found with the "hotel crew."

Hotel crew

To fully understand what a cruise is like, think of it as a hotel that floats. Just as hotels have different personalities and amenities, so do cruises. Some cruises are deluxe, offering the best food and service, similar to staying at an elegant hotel. Other cruises are more casual and fun, filled with activities that cater to a younger crowd.

Whatever style the cruise, most employ crews to work in the following positions:

- Accountant
- Assistant Cruise Director
- Beautician
- Casino Operator
- Cruise Director

- Cruise Staff/Activities
- Disk Jockey
- Doctor/Nurse
- Entertainer
- Gift Shop Manager/Assistant
- Port Lecturer
- Photographer
- Purser
- Reservationist
- Sales Manager
- Shore Excursions Director
- Sports/Fitness Director
- Stewards
- Youth Counselor
- Waiters/Waitresses

Job titles and responsibilities vary from ship to ship. For example, the term "cruise staff" often is synonymous with assistant cruise director, social director, or activities director.

What it's like to be part of a cruise staff

Although filled with its share of excitement and glamour, working on a ship involves hard work. Cruise staff put in long hours—anywhere from eight to fifteen hours a day, seven days a week—and must maintain a high level of energy and always be cordial and friendly to passengers.

Cruise staff members generally are involved with organizing activities and social events, including common shipboard games such as shuffleboard and ring toss, Bingo, aerobics classes, basketball, golf putting (and driving—off the stern of the ship), and pool games. They also participate in cocktail parties and masquerade balls and take every opportunity to make sure passengers feel comfortable and are enjoying themselves.

Many of the cruise staff also double as entertainers and need to have some talent for performing, whether as singers, musicians or DJs.

When in port, most of the crew is allowed to go ashore and have time off to explore, although some cruise staff function as chaperones, helping passengers find their way around foreign locales.

The pleasures and pressures of the job

Activities onboard ship usually follow a rigid schedule, with little time in between for the crew to rest and take a break. With a constant eye on their watches, cruise staff run from one activity to another, announcing games over the loudspeaker, setting up the deck for exercise classes, supervising ring toss tournaments or other special events, and encouraging everyone to participate.

An outgoing, energetic individual would be in his or her element in such a job; someone who lacks those skills would find the work difficult.

The rewards, the pay, and the perks

While salaries are not overly generous, the additional benefits are. Cruise staff are provided with free housing while onboard ship and all they can eat. It's not necessary for a full-time employee of a cruise line to maintain quarters ashore, and therefore, most of the salary can be saved.

Cruise ships also sail to exotic ports, giving staff members the chance to travel and meet people from all over the world.

Climbing the ladder

Assistant cruise directors and other cruise staff can move up the ladder to more supervisory and managerial positions. They need to demonstrate that they have organizational skills, that they can delegate and manage people. They also have to be good at detail work and paper work.

Sometimes earning a promotion has to do with how much experience you have, how good you are—or who has quit or died. As one assistant cruise director pointed out, "It's a good job and most people, once in, don't want to leave."

Getting started

A college education is not necessary, but some cruise lines prefer to see an applicant with a degree in psychology, hotel management, physical education or communications. It's also a good idea to know another language, especially Spanish or German.

Let's Meet...

Beverley Citron
Assistant Cruise Director

Beverley Citron began working on cruise ships at the age of twenty-one as a hairdresser. She also worked as a sports director, then was promoted to assistant cruise director.

What got you interested in working for the cruise industry?

I've wanted to work on a ship since I was five years old. I was influenced by two of my uncles who were in the English Royal Navy. Every time they came ashore they'd show me home movies they'd taken of the blue waters of Australia or Hong Kong. All through my school years it was my goal.

What did you do to prepare for a career with a cruise line?

I worked as a social director for a holiday resort and my local sailing club in England looking after children, planning and implementing their activities. I studied singing and the guitar, then put together an act with musical arrangements and costumes. I was determined to get a job as a social staff member.

How did you feel when you got offered your first job?

After all those years of applying—when I got that letter in the mail saying "Beverley, we have selected you to be a youth counselor...we'll be sending you an air ticket...please get your visa sorted out...," I was literally speechless. That was probably the happiest moment of my life.

What are the duties of assistant cruise directors?

The cruise staff are in charge of all the games, activities and shore excursions for the passengers. In a way, it's similar to being a camp counselor, but for adults. Youth counselors, of course, work with children.

We make sure the passengers are having fun, and we try to come up with activities and events to capture their interest. We might organize a grandmother's tea or give an origami (paper folding) demonstration or stage a treasure hunt. When in port, we might chaperone a group of passengers on a tour. Even between scheduled activities, we interact and socialize constantly with the passengers.

What do you like most about your job?

Working on a cruise ship is my dream job. Every morning I always looked forward to getting up and starting the day.

I'm not an office person, it's very difficult for me to stay at a desk all day. I've got a lot of energy and it's great for me being able to move about the ship making lots of friends, being busy. The people you work with become like a family. Sometimes you have to share a cabin and you become close.

What Made It All Worthwhile

There is a memorable moment for Beverley Citron, something that let her know her choice of career with the cruise industry had been the right one.

Years ago when she started as a youth counselor, there was a little ten-year-old boy who came on the ship with his parents maybe twice a year for three years. He stayed by her side the whole time, always interested, always asking if he could help. When she was off duty, he'd beg his mother to take him to meet her for tea.

The years went by and Beverley lost touch with him. Later, when she was working in a school to train cruise personnel, one of the other teachers took a group of trainees on tour of a ship. Beverley met one of the ship's assistant cruise directors and asked him to show her trainees around. After the tour, the floor was opened to questions. Someone wanted to know how he had gotten involved with this kind of work.

He told them how he had started going on cruises at the age of ten, and that he had been influenced strongly by one lady he'd never forget. "She got me interested in cruising", he told the trainees. "I stuck to her like a stamp to a letter, trying to learn everything I could. I told her that one day I'd be working on a ship and here I am."

The other teacher asked what the lady's name was and he told her—Beverley Citron. The teacher arranged a reunion. Beverley felt so good knowing that she had influenced someone like that.

Let's Meet...

Richard Turnwald
Purser

Rich Turnwald has been working in the cruise industry for more than fourteen years. He started out shoreside, then worked his way up the ranks from junior purser to chief purser.

What first attracted you to a career in the cruise industry?

Ever since I was a little boy I've always loved ships and the sea. I read about them and studied them and there was no doubt in my mind that I wanted to be involved in some way with ships as a profession.

How did you go about getting your first job?

I was in college in Michigan studying travel and tourism and I wanted to get involved with the cruise lines. I sent out my resume and wrote to the various cruise lines, most of which were based in Miami. I was interviewed over the telephone and was offered a position in the office. It was exciting and scary at the same time. I was just out of college and I had to relocate to a place where I didn't know anyone, but it was like a dream for me to be able to work closely with the cruise ships.

What are the duties of a purser?

The purser's office is like the front desk at a big hotel. The staff handle all the money on the ship, they pay all the bills and the salaries, they cash traveler's checks for passengers, provide the safes for the valuables, fill out all the documentation for customs and immigration officials in the different countries, and all the other crucial behind-the-scenes functions.

Passengers come to the purser for information or help with problems. They are in charge of cabin assignments, and they coordinate with the medical personnel to help handle any emergencies.

There are various ranks for a purser: junior or assistant purser, second purser, first purser, then chief purser. As chief purser I had a staff of six people I was responsible for; on larger ships the purser's office might have fourteen or fifteen people.

How regularly do promotions come?

Promotions are based on how well you do your job as well as the length of time you've been employed. I was fortunate. Within three months, I had worked my way up from junior purser to chief purser. Usually it takes a good year or so. It depends on how many people are ahead of you, if they leave or stay.

It can be competitive. You have to consider that there's only one chief purser on each ship. Some people start working on a ship and their only background was watching "The Love Boat." They don't have a realistic viewpoint of the downsides of cruise work.

The First-Day Fiasco

Rich Turnwald writes a letter home about his first day as chief purser, a day he'll never forget.

Dear Mom and Dad,

Today was my first day and first thing, I got a call from one of the stewards, and a water pipe had broken and flooded one of the cabins. It was a deluxe cabin, a suite. The passengers were prominent people, a doctor and his wife, and they had paid thousands of dollars for the cruise. Everything in their cabin was soaked, ruined—probably over $7,000 worth of damage.

I had to go down and try to placate the couple—as you might imagine, they were screaming, and upset. We had to make out an itemized list of everything they owned with their approximate values, because, of course, the cruise line would reimburse them. At the same time, I had to coordinate another cabin for them—luckily we weren't booked fully.

I had the authority to offer more amenities as a gesture of goodwill, such as unlimited wine at dinner and free shore excursions, etc. It was the beginning of the cruise and they had nothing to wear. Other passengers heard about the damage and tried to help by loaning them some clothing. We also gave them free credit at the ship's boutiques.

We were able to soothe them and get them outfitted for the gala and everything went well. Eventually, everyone was able to see some of the humor in the situation. I did learn a lot, though, about dealing with emergencies and that the key is getting everyone to cooperate and help.

I hope my next letter will have less to report!

Love,

Rich

Success Stories

Edwin Stephan

Edwin Stephan, president of Royal Carribean Cruise Line, became interested in the cruise industry when it was in its infancy. He brought many innovative ideas to the business, including building more luxurious ships, opening up deck space, moving dining rooms from below to sea level, and building shipboard atriums with glass elevators, lush foliage, and sweeping staircases.

He also helped establish shorter cruises. Prior to that, most cruises were long-haul events, crossing the Atlantic or traveling around the world. Royal Caribbean began offering two- and three-day and seven-day jaunts, with more affordable fares. Royal Caribbean is the world's largest cruise brand by passenger capacity and operates nine modern ships.

Richard Branson

In 1986, Richard Branson crossed the Atlantic by speedboat in the fastest recorded time ever. He then became the first to cross the Atlantic and Pacific oceans by hot air balloon.

But these achievements are minor compared to everything else Richard Branson has done. He left school at the age of 16 and made his first million one year later. Among his innovative creations are *Student* magazine, Virgin Records, and Virgin Atlantic Airways.

Find Out More

You and being a cruise staff member

Take a look at this typical schedule of an activities director or assistant cruise director. Decide if you could keep up.

8:00	Up and having breakfast
8:30	To the sports deck to make sure tapes are set up for aerobics classes
9:00	Teach the class for 30 minutes
9:30	Sign up passengers for shuffleboard tournament
9:45	Supervise tournament
10:45	Sign up passengers for ring toss
11:00	Teach passengers how to play ring toss
11:30	Socialize with passengers
12:00	Lunch break, then do paperwork or take short nap
2:00	Sports deck for informal play, explain rules of various games and continue to announce upcoming events
3:00	Basketball game
3:45	Get tapes ready for afternoon aerobics class
4:00	Teach aerobics
4:30	Pack up sports deck for the day
5:00	Get showered and dressed for cocktail party

5:10   Attend cocktail party
6:30   Dinner break
7:30   Get ready for evening bingo
       game
8:00   Supervise bingo game
10:00 Dancing under the stars
12:00 Midnight buffet

**Find out
more about
working for
a cruise line**

Cruise Line International
    Association
500 5th Avenue
Suite 1407
New York, NY 10110

*How To Get A Job with A Cruise
    Line.*
by Mary Fallon Miller

Ticket to Adventure Publishing,
P.O. Box 41005,
St. Petersburg, FL 33743-1005.

Includes descriptions of all the
various jobs, an inside look at the
the different cruise lines, interviews with cruise personnel, and
valuable tips on how to go about
getting a job.

FOREIGN
SERVICE
OFFICER

A career serving your country overseas can offer excitement, challenge, and even glamour. As a member of the Foreign Service, which is under the jurisdiction of the U.S. Department of State, you can travel the world, and, at the same time, gain the satisfaction of helping other people and representing the interests of your country.

Being a part of the Foreign Service is more than just a job. It is a complete way of life that requires dedication and commitment. If you're smart and tough enough to get the job done, the Foreign Service might just be the right place for you.

Different positions within the Foreign Service

The Foreign Service divides the different specialty areas into the following "cones":

Administration

Administrative personnel at overseas posts are responsible for hiring foreign national workers, providing office and residential space, assuring reliable communications with Washington, D.C., supervising computer systems, and–of great importance in hostile or unfriendly areas–providing security for the post's personnel and property.

Consular Services

Consular workers often must combine the skills of lawyers, judges, investigators, and social workers. Their duties range from issuing passports and visas, to finding a lost child, or helping a traveler in trouble.

Economic Officers

Economic officers maintain contact with key business and financial leaders in the host country and report to Washington on the local economic conditions and their impact on American trade and investment policies. They are concerned with issues such as commercial aviation safety, fishing rights, and international banking.

Political Affairs

Those working in political affairs analyze and report on the political views of the host country. They make contact with labor unions, humanitarian organizations, educators, and cultural leaders.

Information and Cultural Affairs

As part of the Foreign Service, the U.S. Information Agency (USIA) promotes cultural, informational, and public diplomacy programs. An Information Officer might develop a library open to the public, meet with the press, and oversee English language training programs for the host country.

Commercial and Business Services

In this division, a Foreign Service Officer identifies overseas business connections for American exporters and investors, conducts market research for the success of U.S. products, and organizes trade shows and other promotional events.

What it's like being a Foreign Service Officer

Foreign Service Officers can be based in Washington D.C. or can be sent anywhere in the world. They work at embassies, consulates, and other diplomatic missions in major cities or small towns. They help the thousands of Americans traveling and living overseas, issue visas to citizens of other countries wishing to visit the

United States, and help our government execute our foreign policies.

The Foreign Service Officer accepts direction from the President of the United States and his top appointees. The main goal is to make U.S. policies succeed. He or she is expected to place loyalty over personal opinions and preferences.

The pleasures and pressures

Foreign Service workers can experience a glamorous lifestyle, dining with their ambassador in luxurious places, meeting royalty, or other heads of state. They can be present at important decision-making sessions and influence world politics and history.

But postings can offer hardship as well, in environments as hostile as Antarctica or a Middle Eastern desert. Some assignments, or postings, are in isolated locations without all the familiar comforts of home. The weather can be harsh, and there can be health hazards. Danger from unrest or war is possible. In spite of the difficulties, those in the Foreign Service are happy with the unique rewards and opportunities.

The rewards the pay, the perks

The starting salary generally is low, but it may be increased at overseas posts with free housing, furniture and utilities, travel expenses, educational allowances for children, and cost-of-living allowances in high-cost cities.

Extra pay is given for dangerous and "hardship" posts.

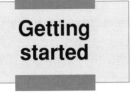

Getting started

Although many Foreign Service Officers are skilled in political science and history, these days candidates can have knowledge in specialized fields such as the environment, computer science, the fight against AIDS, antidrug efforts, and trade.

There are several steps to complete in order to apply for a position in the Foreign Service:

Written Examination

This is a day-long multiple-choice test usually given once a year. It measures verbal and numerical reasoning, political and cultural awareness, English-language expression, and knowledge of topics important to the function of the Foreign Service. It's a difficult exam and many people have to take it more than once before they pass.

Oral Evaluation

Those who pass the written exam will be invited to participate in an all-day Oral Assessment. It tests the skills, abilities, knowledge, and personal characteristics necessary to succeed in the Foreign Service. Writing skills are measured, as well as administrative, problem-solving, leadership, and interpersonal skills.

Medical Clearance

Because many postings have inadequate health care or pose health hazards, candidates for the Foreign Service must meet a high medical standard. Allowances are made, however, for certain handicaps.

Background Investigation

The Department of State, along with other federal, state and local agencies, conducts a thorough background check on Foreign Service candidates. They examine employment records, credit history, repayment of school loans, drug abuse, and criminal records.

Eligibility

Before you can take the Foreign Service Written Examination you must be:

- at least 20 years old on the date of the exam
- no more than 59 years old
- a citizen of the United States
- available for worldwide assignment

Things you can do to get a head start

The following suggestions will help prepare you for a career in the Foreign Service: Do well in school, go to college and get a well-rounded education, read the newspaper regularly, and be aware of issues that concern our country.

Let's Meet...

Jim Van Laningham
General Services Officer

Jim Van Laningham has made the Foreign Service his career for more than fifteen years.

What attracted you to the Foreign Service?

Originally, I became interested about the time I was in junior high school. I had just read the book, *The Ugly American,* and it talked about the image of Americans overseas and how Foreign Service Officers helped correct what often was a bad image. It got me thinking about it. Eventually I took the Foreign Service exam and I got in.

What did you study to prepare yourself?

I earned a bachelor's degree in economics, then went on for a master's in international business. I took the exam right after I graduated and all the information was still fresh. My education was helpful.

What happened after you took the exam?

It was a year and half from the time I took the exam until I got accepted. I was very excited. They called me up one day and asked if I could be there in less than a month. They wanted an answer right away. My wife and I discussed it and decided to take the plunge. We went to Washington and they gave me about two months of training in a basic orientation course for new officers and six months of language training.

After that, I was assigned to the embassy in Moscow as an economics officer. Today it's almost mandatory that the first tour for most Foreign Service Officers is as a consular officer, issuing visas to people who want to come to the United States.

What special skills do you think someone needs to be a good Foreign Service Officer?

You have to be able to write well, to organize thoughts logically and coherently. You have to be outgoing and have people-skills. I think you have to be interested in the world and what's going on around you, because a lot of what you do is reporting back to Washington on what's happening in the country you're in. And if you're in the administration cone, hopefully you are a good manager of people. You have to have leadership ability. It also helps to be familiar with finances and budgets.

But I don't think there's any one particular field of study that leads to the Foreign Service. The people I've met have taken every imaginable major in school. It's more just studying well and getting a well-rounded education.

Jim Van Laningham's Long-Distance Class Reunion

Jim was posted in Iraq at the time Saddam Hussein invaded Kuwait. He had been scheduled to fly home to attend his high school reunion, but there were no planes leaving the country and he couldn't get out.

They were able to evacuate most of the staff of the American embassy in Baghdad, and had about one hundred people from the embassy in Kuwait who were trying to get back to the United States. Although they were given permission to leave, it turned out they were not able to. A lot of his time was spent trying to get exit visas. The permission finally came through at about three o'clock in the morning, Iraqi time.

Jim suddenly remembered that that was the exact time his high school reunion had been scheduled. He knew the telephone number where the reunion was being held, so he called and ended up talking to about 40 of his former classmates over the phone. Between that and having had just succeeded in getting visas for a hundred people to get out of the country, it made a wonderful experience, one that Jim won't forget.

Let's Meet...

Robert Manzanares
Administrative Officer

Bob Manzanares has held the positions of Consular Officer, General Services Officer, Chief of Post Management for the Middle Eastern Bureau, and Director for the Office of Administration for the National Security Council.

What first attracted you to a career in the Foreign Service?

While I was in graduate school studying public administration, I met a State Department employee. He had just served in Peru and spoke perfect Spanish. I was amazed at his language capabilities because, even with my Hispanic background, he was showing me up badly. I asked him how he had become so proficient and he told me about the Foreign Service.

I was attracted to all the stories he told, the languages, the cultures, the travel, and on a lark I decided to take the test, not thinking I would pass. I didn't pass the first time. I tried again and then I was successful.

Most people start out as a Consular Officer. Can you tell us what that's like?

I was a Consular Officer in Mexico City, which was known as a "visa mill." Everyone wanted to come to the United States and by eight o'clock in the morning we would have between two and three thousand people waiting in this huge line to enter the compound and apply for a visa. I was one of fourteen officers working in a little *casita,* a makeshift hut, and we would listen to each applicant for a minute to a minute and a half and make a decision whether or not to issue a visa. This would go on non-stop from eight to two and we would process more than 4,000 applications a day. In the afternoon we would issue visas with passports that came in through a tourist agency. It was the same work, but not as interesting because we didn't get to talk to the people.

I also made prison visits. Occasionally, we have Americans who wind up in prison, for whatever reasons, and so my job was to go in and make sure they were not being abused and that they had access to an attorney. Also, if an American should die overseas, the consular officer has to contact the family and make arrangements to ship the body home.

What were some of your duties when you were Chief of Post Management for the Middle Eastern Bureau in Washington?

I was one of the main organizers–from the logistical side–of the Middle East Peace Talks that took place in Madrid. Working with a team, I organized the conference site and coordinated all the different arrangements for a conference: security, transportation, hotels, interpreters, etc.

Don't Forget Your Country

Bob Manzanares is patriotic about the United States. Sometimes he's reminded of how much he loves his country when he's been overseas for a year or eighteen months and hasn't been home in all that time. When Bob and his staff expect a Congressional delegation or a Presidential visit and he sees that American plane coming in with the "United States of America" painted on its side and the big American flag on the back, it brings chills up his spine.

Bob also sees the host country's people in awe of what we have in the United States, and it makes him wish that Americans could learn to appreciate their own country more.

Success Stories

Shirley Temple

Who hasn't watched an old black-and-white movie on a Sunday afternoon starring the adorable 1930s child actress, Shirley Temple? Her dimpled smile and curly hair first captivated America during the Depression. Her movies–Heidi, Rebecca of Sunnybrook Farm, Little Miss Marker, The Little Colonel, and Wee Willie Winkie, to name just a few–still delight audiences today with her singing (remember *On the Goodship Lollipop*?), tap dancing, and fetching manner.

Shirley Temple's film career ended in 1949 after a series of unremarkable teenage and adult roles. She emerged twenty years later as Shirley Temple Black and served as a delegate to the United Nations in 1969 and as U.S. Ambassador to Ghana in 1974. In 1976 President Gerald Ford appointed her as U.S. Chief of Protocol, and in 1989 President George Bush appointed her as U.S. Ambassador to Czechoslovakia.

Henry Kissinger

The U.S. Secretary of State is responsible for the entire Foreign Service. Henry Kissinger was chief foreign policy advisor and secretary of state to Presidents Richard Nixon and Gerald Ford. In these positions he was able to attain an unusual amount of power and prestige.

Find Out More

Department of State
Recruitment Division
P.O. Box 9317
Rosslyn Station
Arlington, VA 22209

ENGLISH AS A

FOREIGN LANGUAGE

(EFL) TEACHER

I t's estimated that more than one thousand million people around the world speak or are studying how to speak English. They choose to learn English for a number of reasons: to attend colleges and universities in English-speaking countries, for business, for employment, for government relations, for travel, or to be able to communicate day-to-day in the English-speaking country in which they live.

The need for teachers is increasing, and so are the locations in which they can work. Teachers of English as a foreign language (EFL) work overseas with students from other cultures and language backgrounds. Teachers of English as a second language (ESL) generally work in the United States, teaching students who have come to study, work, or live here.

Where EFL teachers work

EFL teachers find employment almost anywhere, although the largest concentration of jobs appears to be in Middle Eastern countries (Saudi Arabia, Oman, and Jordan), in the Far Eastern countries (Japan, Hong Kong, China, and South Korea), in eastern Europe (Turkey and Poland), in North Africa (Algeria, Egypt, and Morocco), and in other regions of Africa and South America.

EFL teachers find work in private or government-funded language centers, in international schools, and in universities and colleges. EFL teachers also can find part-time work tutoring individuals.

What an EFL teacher does

EFL teachers instruct students in the basic English language skills, such as reading, writing, listening, and conversation. Like any teachers, they are responsible for designing lesson plans and for administering and grading tests. They also might help design curriculum and write materials to be used in the classroom.

The students EFL teachers instruct could be children in

primary or secondary schools, university age, or adults.

The pleasures and pressures of the job

To most EFL teachers, the main pleasure of the profession is not just the opportunity to travel, but the chance to live for long periods of time in a variety of foreign countries. EFL teachers also enjoy the benefits of shorter working days and long summer vacations.

But being away from home for long periods of time also has its disadvantages. Even though it's easy to make new friends, it's possible to feel cut off from family and friends at home. You might not be able to follow local politics or your favorite baseball team, television programs come and go, and all the products with which you're familiar might not be available.

Many EFL teachers, however, make working abroad a way of life. Their stays range from one to ten years, or even longer. That is proof of how much they are enjoying themselves.

The rewards, the pay, and the

Salaries and benefits vary from region to region and employer to employer. In general, jobs in areas that offer more "hardship" to Americans, such as the Middle East, pay higher wages and provide many special allowances. You would receive free housing and furniture, free travel, free medical care, and a bonus at the end of your contract.

In poorer countries or in countries where the lifestyle is more compatible with what Americans are used to, salaries are lower.

No matter in which country you work, if you meet certain requirements, such as the length of time spent out of the United States, you will not be required to pay U.S. income tax.

Getting started

Many people not yet in the profession think, "I can speak English, therefore I can teach it." In some places, that's true, and often, travelers wanting to earn extra money to help pay for their trip find work tutoring or providing practice in conversation skills. But as the number of professionally trained teachers increases, opportunities for unqualified teachers decrease.

These days, a bachelor's degree is considered the minimum qualification for teaching EFL. A master's degree would be necessary to teach in a university setting. State certification as a teacher is required for those teaching in American schools and some international schools.

Teacher trainees study methodology, second language acquisition, curriculum design, computer-assisted language learning, and research methods.

Climbing the career ladder

EFL teachers can move up three different ladders. Some choose to spend most of their time designing curriculum and materials or writing textbooks. Others devote their time to training new teachers. Still others move into administrative positions and become coordinators or directors.

Now decide if a career in EFL is right for you

Do you have the following qualities? Check off the ones that apply to you, then decide which are the most important to be a successful EFL teacher.

__ I like to meet people from different cultures.

__ I'm not afraid to travel by myself.

__ I can work as part of a team.

__ I have a lot of patience.

__ I don't expect other people to act or think the way I do.

__ I'm curious about how people learn languages.

__ I like to find creative ways to get my point across.

__ I can live without my favorite television programs.

__ I'm not afraid to try new foods.

__ I can adapt to new customs.

Were you able to check off all of the above qualities? Good. Then teaching EFL might just be the career for you.

Let's Meet...

James McMullan
EFL Teacher

James McMullan started teaching EFL in 1978, right after he graduated from the University of London with a bachelor's degree in English. He has lived and worked in England, Germany, Nigeria, Egypt, Qatar, Oman, Yemen, and California.

Tell us about your first job.

It was a lucky break that I got the job. A professor at my college knew that I wanted to go overseas and he mentioned that there was an opening at a university in Germany. Another teacher had dropped out at the last moment.

It was my first trip away from England, my home country, and I was excited when I got the job. I was just twenty-one, fresh out of college, and the students I was teaching were my own age or a little bit younger.

I was a *Lektor,* an assistant teacher. From twelve to fourteen hours a week I taught basic courses such as grammar, literature, and some translation.

What do you like most about the EFL profession?

The opportunity to get to know people from other cultures closely, as well as imparting something they consider of value, which is the English language. You can get a lot back learning about the different ways people look at things.

The employment package working over-seas also is attractive, with allowances for accommodation, transportation, and health, among other benefits. It's a good way to save some money. And as with any teaching position, especially in a university setting, you tend to have a lot of leisure time for exploring the country.

What do you like least about the profession?

Unless you're very dedicated to the language side or you move up professionally into more administrative duties, I don't see it as a profession for life. It's a young people's profes-sion; it can lose its attraction, the longer you do it. After twenty years or so overseas, you can get burned out. However, those first few years tend to be very rewarding and broaden-ing. I feel I had wonderful experiences.

What can someone do to avoid getting burned out?

It's a good idea to develop an interest in which you can move sideways. Teaching EFL makes you a good communicator, and as a result, you will be good at communicating any other body of knowledge: management training, career and cross-cultural counsel-ing, and job skills preparation. I know many EFL teachers who have gone on to become writers or journalists.

What is the most difficult part of your job?

Learning to be flexible, and tailoring what you have to offer to what your employer and the students need. You have to adapt to the constraints of the particular country.

Tips for Writing a Winning Cover Letter

When it comes time to start job hunting, James McMullan suggests that a neat, organized resume and a good cover letter will help attract attention. Here are a few guidelines to follow:

1. Don't write form letters. Each letter must be personally addressed to the employer and should be tailor-made for each specific job. A word processor makes the task easier.

2. Don't ramble. keep your cover letter short and to the point, but remember to mention your most relevant experience or qualifications right up front. Those are your selling points, the reasons that particular school or university will want to hire you.

3. Never apologize or make excuses for your lack of experience. If you express any doubts in your ability to do the job, the employer will, no doubt, feel the same.

4. Neatness counts. Your letter should be perfect. No strikeovers, blobs or correction fluid, typos, spelling mistakes, or grammatical errors. If you send in a messy cover letter or resume, the employer will assume that that's the kind of work he can expect from you.

5. Don't use colorful or cute stationery. A good bond paper, the same paper you have used for your resume, will work for your cover letter as well.

6. Keep the tone of your letter friendly but formal.

7. Don't mention the resume you've attached until you're ready to sign off. If you refer to it too soon, the reader will turn to it before finishing your letter.

8. Make known your availability for an interview, but remember to be flexible. The employer is not interested in your exam schedule or dentist appointment.

Let's Meet...

Deborah Gordon
EFL Teacher/Coordinator

Deborah Gordon began her career as an EFL professional in 1972. She's worked in Massachusetts, Iran, Madagascar, Spain, England, New Mexico, Texas, Hawaii, and the Sultanate of Oman.

How did you get started in EFL?

Originally I was studying prelaw, EFL wasn't something I had thought of or pursued actively. I was volunteering at a welfare center and there was a need for teachers. I was asked if I could help out. My students were Hispanic children in their young teens. I enjoyed the work and discovered I was interested in learning languages. I got exposed to EFL when I went to Spain to study Spanish. EFL seemed a good way to travel and experience other cultures.

What special training do you have in this field?

I have a bachelor's degree in liberal arts/comparative literature and a master's degree in teaching English as a second language. I also took an EFL teacher training course in England.

The courses I studied included second language acquisition, methodology, how to teach the individual skill areas–reading, writing, listening, and speaking–testing, curriculum design, and research methods.

What special skills or qualities should someone have to be an EFL teacher?

You need to be a "people-person," a good listener, and have a lot of patience. You need to be flexible and reach past your own cultural upbringing so that you can understand the people you're working with. Also, you need to be creative and energetic so you can capture your students' interest.

Is it necessary to know another language to teach EFL?

It's not necessary but it's useful. Most EFL teachers teach directly English to English. If you work in the United States, you'll have classes with students from many different countries and it won't help you if you know one or two languages.

However, it is helpful to study a language, because it lets you understand the problems people encounter when they're trying to learn English. And when you're overseas, it helps you communicate more effectively in a foreign country.

What do you like most about being a coordinator?

I enjoy the opportunity to design a program of my own and implement it. I love writing materials and designing curriculum. It's satisfying for me to see that through.

A Typical Work Week for Deborah Gordon in Oman

Saturday	(which, in the Arab World, is equivalent to Monday, the first day of the week.): Make a schedule for my work for the week, edit classroom materials before taking them to the printer, have a meeting with other teachers. After work go with the family to the staff club swimming pool.
Sunday:	Design an exam to be given the next day, teach a class in technical report writing, meet with teachers in my program, write up the minutes of the meeting, and work on more materials. After work, play a game of squash.
Monday:	Teach a class in reading comprehension, give a test in another class, more meetings, edit materials written by other teachers. After work, a trip to the vegetable *souk* (market).
Tuesday:	Grade test papers, teach speaking and listening classes covering giving and getting permission, meet with professors in other departments. Dinner gathering with friends in the evening.
Wednesday:	Order books, write course reports and evaluations, input grades into the computer, hold office hours for students. In the evening stay home and watch videos.
Thursday	(Equivalent to a Saturday): go to the fish *souk* early in the morning and purchase fish off the boats. Head off on a camping trip, exploring wadis (dry river beds) or mountains.
Friday:	Come back from a day-trip and in the evening meet with friends for dinner.

Success Stories

Peace Corps The Peace Corps was established in the early 1960s by John F. Kennedy, who was the president of the United States at that time. Kennedy did not want his administration to be a giant flexing its muscles in the face of communism. He wanted to find a nonthreatening way to influence the world and to ensure good relations between the United States and developing countries. The Peace Corps was the answer. With more than 100,000 volunteers (Kennedy's "Soldiers of Peace") since its beginning days in the early 1960s, the Peace Corps combines friendship with practical assistance, such as farming techniques, English-language training, and technological expertise (for example, modern farming methods). The Peace Corps is still going strong.

Charles Berlitz Charles Berlitz is the grandson of Maximilian Berlitz, who established the first Berlitz School in 1878 in Providence, Rhode Island. Since then, over 6,000 instructors have taught more than 100,000 students in Berlitz language schools around the world. Charles Berlitz speaks more than thirty languages. He came from a multilingual family. With the "Berlitz Method," the instructor uses only the subject language in the classroom, identifying objects and acting out situations. Many famous actors, diplomats, and politicians have studied under Berlitz.

Find Out More

What are all those abbreviations?

People who are unfamiliar with the profession can get confused by all the acronyms, many of which are used interchangeably.

TESOL Teaching English to Speakers of Other Languages

Used in the U.S. to refer to the degree you earn to become a teacher in the field. For example, you can work toward a master's degree or a certificate in TESOL.

ESL English as a Second Language

Used for programs conducted in English-speaking countries where students might live and work but do not speak English as a first language.

EFL English as a Foreign Language

Used for programs in non-English-speaking countries where students need to know English for business or tourism.

TESL/TEFL Teaching English as a Second Language or as a Foreign Language

Used to refer to ESL/EFL programs in the United Kingdom or in other English-speaking countries outside the U.S. The terms also refer to the degree or certificate teachers obtain in countries other than the United States. For example, you can earn a diploma or certificate in TESL/TEFL.

ESOL English to Speakers of Other Languages

Used for programs in elementary and secondary schools in the U.S.

TOEFL The Test of English as a Foreign Language

Administered around the world to students applying to U.S. universities.

Find out more about TESOL

Teachers of English to Speakers of Other Languages, Inc. (TESOL)
1600 Cameron Street
Suite 300
Alexandria, VA 22314-2705

INDEX